1

ISBN: 978-198-336-3481

First printed in Great Britain 2018

Second Edition, printed in Great Britain 2019

Copyright © 2018 Arch Hades

Photographs by Arch Hades

The cure for love is to be loved back
- Friedrich Nietzsche

Poetry & Postcards

Volume 1

High Tide

Index

Part 1: Poetry

Part 2: Postcards

Part 1
Poetry

There's nothing quite like your first high
I'll chase forever, you and I

Summer rain, I feel your rush
Heartache hits at our first touch

Midnight

Nowhere I'd rather be
It's not a place, it's a feeling,
This paradise you give me

Son of a preacher man

My desert rain,
You fill my lungs
Kiss away my pain
And speak in tongues

My fever dream,
You help me soar
To such great heights
I so adore

My neon night,
Makes me feel young
As if tomorrow
Will never come

Higher and higher

Give me your magic, I want to feel it in my veins
Surround me, I want to feel you break my chains

How much I want to give you all my secrets
I know you'll keep them safe

Spark

Sheer lightness of your being
While others burn, you shine
There's no decay about you
This piercing glow, sublime

Silently, you rise above
A calmness in your wake
This purity unbound
Always giving, with no take

And if your light goes out
I ache to be that spark
To reignite, you'll never,
Have to feel the dark

Say you do

I see the light, I feel the heat
The numbing, soft embrace
Eternity, welcoming me,
Undressed by golden haze

Take my hand and lift me up
Show me to heaven's door
Your dazzling white entwines
Panacea cures once more

Adore

London, 00:42, Friday

I want you, all of you. I want your late nights and your black outs at 3am. I want you to sleep in my bed and I want you to call it home. I want your phone calls and your excuses. I want to wait for you no matter how late you arrive. I want to make you laugh. I want your bad days and your worst. I want to dance in your car and catch your smile. I want you, all of you.

On Top

To run away with you, would be
My crowning dream come true
You're all I've ever wanted, needed
All my hopes you've far exceeded
A love so easy, yet divine
You simply make me feel alive

Ashton

Stripped fearless while sailing
Submerged in light alone
A storm had swept both oceans
Your fate with darkness sown

A fervid zeal that brewed within
A first-rate madness set
Unleashed, at last, from a solivagant
Your arcane song, now a duet

That agile crest you mastered
You turned against the tide
A yen for the extraordinary
Forever fills your stride

Ahead you soar with ardour
Nostalgia in your trails
Ebullient, unstoppable
High spirits in your sails

On reflection, I think that's what love is,
all the things I used to enjoy on my own,
I now want to share with you

Cocoon

You stretch afar
I stand and watch

It's been too long, but I can wait
You turn, unfold, unfurl and grow

Around you, time stands still
You're not controlled by anything

My eyes believe you filled the oceans
And made the mountains rise

Deceive me however many times
My heart is yours to break

My love, my soul's home in human form

If I were a painter, I'd paint the world for you
But I only have my words so I'll use them all on you

White nights

You rise and rise with grandeur
You rise away from me
Triumphant, shimmering in splendour,
I watch you surge with glee

The sunset paints us amaranth
With persimmon high hopes
Carnation, lavender, pompadour
And heliotrope slopes

The sea beneath you glimmers
And lusters with rich shades
Of tyrian, vermillion,
Crimson, rose cascades

The dusk is fast approaching
The colours still ablaze,
Twilight almost here,
Dispersing Tuscan haze

And still you rise with glory,
With calm divinity
I stand elated, watching,
Your voyage to infinity

These little hearts are bound to break
And when they do, their demons wake

Grand Haven

I'm losing sleep to hear you breathe
My desperate love keeps me awake
Adoring you with every heave
My aching heart, no more can take

Your 'soon' too often meant just never
Casting aside my envelopes
You didn't mean it when you said forever
You'll never give me more than hope

So play my heartstrings,
Strum them till they break
Your strange disease upon me
Your rosary around my neck

I can't give you the whole world,
But I can give you mine
I'll swear my love into your silence
While I pretend I'm fine

You were never mine to begin with

Daisies

I imagined us so often
It felt like a memory

Alone, your presence
Filled my reverie

But felt so lonely
In your company

Always awaiting
→ Redamancy

*— The act
of loving
in return*

Fading

Drowning in my thoughts
At the bottom of your sea
Before I dissolve, hurry
And come back to me

The killing moon

And when I hear your voice once more
Our kaleidoscope of memories
Turns and pours out from the phone

For this, there is no remedy
A burning mist consumes my eyes
A melancholy ecstasy, why can't these feelings die

You hang up the phone and
oceans appear between us once again

Notion

Intoxicated with sadness
In love with all your madness
Oh, I could overdose on you

You'll delight in my violent end
Stand by, watch me descend,
Savouring the view

The ocean, like you

Caught off-guard by your footsteps
In a crowded room, strangers fade
I resist to return or remember
Yielding, my consciousness sways

Shut my eyes to fool the night-time
Driving ocean side, hand in mine
Crossing all the state-lines,
My smile reflected in your eyes

Saw you first at midnight
That sign was all I needed
Haunted by desire
Entwined, this wreck completed

My future inhabitant of my future dreams
My future nightmares, my everything
The sky was on fire, and so was I
The night we met, my sorrows died

The ocean, like you, a sweet reverie
The ocean, like you, wild and free
Salt in the breeze, the current runs deep
The ocean, like you, never mine to keep

Dominoes

Broken hearts keep breaking others
Holding on to their disdain
Not thinking twice about hurting lovers
When they're already numb to pain

Fanaa (fuh-naa): self-destruction for love

Are you the calm, or are you the storm?
Snared in the eye of your hurricane,
Without knowing how to return

Are you the tempest, or the norm?
My being blisters in your fire,
Your glance glazes as I deform

Are you my freedom, or my keep?
I drown beneath your waves
My grief, so willingly, you reap

Loving you, was the most precious form
Of bittersweet fanaa, I have known
Your gaze like ice, your embrace never warm
I stand behind you, however forlorn

I loved you like Icarus loved the sun
Too much, too close, my wings unspun
And while searching for you, high up above
I lost myself, entranced by this love

Love isn't blind
Love blinds you

Hallelujah

Your medicine, your poison
Poured it down my throat
With tears of my surrender
Quenching both our thirsts

No one's immune to love's disease

Your beautiful game

You never let me get too close.
Your 'omens' taught you otherwise,
You say, in your stern voice.
You say you like these games we play,
But some rules have turned it ugly
Dance if you want, sing along if you want,
Don't stand and stare so smugly
I'm tired of these eggshells,
Your 'cause and effect'
Love's not formulaic
News to you, I suspect
And in your labyrinth
I have no birds-eye view,
I loathe your instructions
Don't preach what to do
You're not an enigma,
My puzzle to solve,
Just a beautiful boy
Who wants my resolve
Anything I do,
I do it all wrong
This is exhausting
And just can't go on

I can't tell if I don't want to lose him,
or if I just don't want to lose

Red skies

Pure molten coals, your hazel eyes
Burning desire in your arms
We coalesce and intertwine
Shaking shivers down my spine

Ferocious fire, turned to ash
Burned out too swiftly, in a flash
The day your glowing coals went cold
Like a house of cards, we fold

Venice

17:31 Friday

In December, you told me I changed your life
Three months later, I asked you one more time
Your eyes avoiding mine,
I knew you'd changed your mind
It was the beginning of our end
And that is how 'we' died

Reckless

The velvet sun sets over us
Bathed in scents of laughter
To hold you once again so close
And never speak thereafter

Love's fever climbs too high for me
Realisation of my fears
I will cry oceans over you
Mourn our parting with my tears

Seabird

Your love was made to measure
But always fit too small
Begging for attention
Your love, so terminal

You'd walk in front of me
Ashamed to hold my hand
Shared glances never softened you
Affection, always banned

You'd introduce me as your friend
My heart would splinter every time
Until a chasm would grow so big
I'd stay at home and sit and cry

You said you'd always love me,
But I know you love her more
It's such a shame that loving me
Became to you, a chore

So much you didn't understand
So thoughtless and so callow
You never met what I needed,
Your love remained too shallow

And soon our time ran out
With you, left all that joy
But I know, without doubt
You're no villain, just a boy

He didn't make the chaos count

Deleted scenes

Shaking and crying, a meter apart
Already forgiving, as you're breaking my heart
I'll do what I can to soften these blows
When you hurt, I hurt, I need you to know
I'll accept when you say – it's not meant to be
And I pray for your happiness, even if it's not me

Our time was only temporary, but you made life less ordinary

Augusta

Sweet emotion, don't fade yet
I'm not finished with this high
Separation, I'll regret
It's too soon to say goodbye

My home and my adventure
Here we stand two broken hearts
Destiny, I censure how
Even good things break apart

Live on

I vividly imagine, your arms around me
Dancing, spinning with your ghost, past realities
At least we're reunited, in my hollow dreams
Warming, worn-out memories, bursting all my seams

I wish we had more time, when we had the chance
My solemn, silent serenade, my hypnotising trance
Even if it's futile, this, I won't regret
You're never fully gone, because I won't forget

Sunsets

You were my constellation,
But now there's a black hole
It'll drag me in, with no salvation,
I'll let it take control

If pain is all that's left of us
I'll let it spear my heart
And even if there is no bright side,
I'll sit here lonesome in the dark

Just when I think I'm on the mend
Catch myself typing out texts
I know I'll never send

My tears of sorrow turn to tears of surrender

Spectre

Stiff at first embrace,
Ebbing softer with submission,
Your arms around me lock

This home, a refuge, I deliquesce
Withal, I fear this our énouement
Sillage, serene and still around me

Like bullets in the night,
My memories of you
Tear through the silence,
Soul's rupture dawns

Once more, I bleed
Your bliss so willingly
This wound won't heal,
Your shadow lingers

Don't go where I can't follow
You spoke to me with words,
I looked at you with love
This paramnesia leaves me hollow

Not contagious

Gifted with infinite rage
Armed with arrows of indifference

Kalopsia:

the delusion of things being more beautiful
than they really are

The devil and angel on my shoulders
They're starting to sound the same
I'll understand maybe when I'm older
When I stop to feel regret and shame

And as another story ends
These lines of right and wrong
They blur then fade away, I wonder
Was I the villain all along?

Everyone's too busy, trying to save themselves

Prophecies

This holy ground, it burns my feet
Why can't this sinner be?
At least don't let me walk alone,
While this fire rages on in me

Shadows

Silence announced your arrival
And it'll linger once you go
Your eclipse consumes this vale
Yet you're delicate, pristine like snow

Long winter reigns, I will withstand
Wild daemons can't distort
Your gift to me, I will accept
Your darkness, I'll absorb

Shadows return, they bind my hands
Show me those northern lights once more
Hand me my armour and my sword,
I know my duty that I swore

I will not run, I will abide
Slow motion dance in your euphoria
Immersing in formaldehyde
Unceasing, black phantasmagoria

My dearest friend

Your theatre of glowing darkness
Without invitation
We'll have to watch the show
Without hesitation

Heads tilt with wonder, crass
This audience participation
Beguiles every heart
Breath drawn, anticipation

If every fear does hide a wish
A want for life immortal
A shared desire of youth
Repulsion from the portal

Death doesn't come a-running
And you can't run away
I'm going nowhere fast
And soon I'll join the fray

You'll hold my hand so gently
Your grip around my waist
We'll waltz into the light
Without undue haste

All costumes come undone
The masks fall to the ground
I am alone, as everyone
Finally, home-bound

Remedy

Full of lies, our plague
The flesh we share
We arise from dust
And produce our heirs

The truth doesn't count
It's the stories we sell
Trapped in our minds
In our own deep wells

Still, our golden hours
Our earth and our salt
We give to each other,
I am no one's fault

The way it was

Flicking through
old photographs of us
I see myself,
smiling less and less

I've grown out of you

Roses

Three times you tried to fan the flames
And twice, they re-ignited
I watch you walk into the room,
My heart, for you, short-sighted

Love, I'm on your side
In your cocoon,
Roses should bloom
However blighted

You wipe my mind of fear,
Of memory and time
My treasured everlasting,
You are the true sublime

The love I want is chaos,
A youthful wanderlust
You touch my hand so tamely
That weak grip, I mistrust

My blood love, once a firework
You lit up my whole sky
I breathed you in and every night
With you, another high

You ask if you should stay
My eyes glance at the door
In love with love, forever
In love with you, no more

Such great heights

If I were to come across
A memory of you
A photograph, a letter,
That book that's overdue
In that object, you'd remain,
As I remember you
You've surely changed now,
Beyond what I once knew

Evanescence

Evanescence of perfection
Your face evades my recollection
To summon you is proving hopeless
With time, you're fading out of focus

You're the ghost in all my stories

Riptide

I wonder if you ever
Wonder about me?
And if you ever wonder
Was it meant to be?

If I still love the Killers
And strawberry iced tea?
If I'm sleeping next to someone
And letting him hold me?

I wonder if you ever
Say aloud my name?
I wonder if you wonder
If I ever do the same?

Our stars were not aligned,
It wasn't meant to be
So if you ever wonder,
Stop wondering 'bout me

Byron

You gave me mornings filled with bird song
And starry evenings, just us two
Constant love throughout the seasons
My heart would harden without you

Otterlo

I want to stand in the forest
Hear the birdsong, smell the pines
I want to shed my human skin
I want to feel the world is mine

Your spring may come too late
Your nettles may sting me
But when your fine air fills my lungs
I'll dissolve, in your serenity

This church of mine

A canopy of summer stars
Hangs loosely in the sky
I am alone and once again,
There's only you and I

My dearest friend,
My every wish and fear,
My pinnacle,
The one I hold so dear

You are eternal,
I'm passing by
Our beings touch,
I feel you're mine

Your love for all still courses
That river never dries,
A steady stream for wonderers,
From all the lows and highs

Your refuge everlasting
Love, unconditional
I, cursed with death
While you, remain transitional

That curse, you've all but lifted
No longer does it sting
With you I stand here gifted,
Before that golden ring

Your bells, your bells ring out
A deafening, silent call
My flaws from me you'll rid
I know you'll break my fall

Eidolon

Race away, eidolon
You're bound by nothing, no one

A mayfly to your aeonian verve
I'll age, I'll die, I'll vanish

You'll sail the world in splendour
At dawn, at dusk, with vigour

I endure to adore you
The most harmonious calm

A soul's high tide
My forever is a moment with you

Tourist

We haven't loved in vain,

Through my memories you'll wander

But just a tourist you'll remain

Nothing more thereafter

Summer nights

Do you still keep our photos, like I do, boxed up?
Too painful to look at, too precious to give up
Does your tattoo remind you, how drunk we used to get?
Wasting summer nights, making crazy bets

You never tried to change me, just quietly adored
I just want to say thank you, I wish I'd told you more

I still think of us, when I hear our final song
We weren't a good match, but brightly we still burned
I hope you don't regret, a single thing we'd done
Because the truth is, I loved you, more than anyone

No one gets the part of me I gave to you

Everyone has loved someone, lost someone,
and can love again

There's no such thing as wasted love

Part 2

Postcards

My Love,

It's windy. I've sought
shelter in a steak house
on the waterfront. These
sunsets, oh, these
sentimental colours,
they are worth it.
This is the furthest I
have been from home.
I don't miss it.

X.

0 E 1 0 1 6   Royal Mail
Jubilee Mail
First Class

1ST

NEW ZEALAND

Wellington, New Zealand

It's windy. I've sought shelter in a steakhouse on the waterfront.

These sunsets, oh, these sentimental colours, they are worth it.

This is the furthest I have been from home. I don't miss it

My Love,
I am writing to you from the Sanderson. Last night, as we strolled home along the embankment, we stopped for a moment to watch a huge stingray silently drift beneath, its' wings licking the stonework. I felt its presence.

A.   081016

Royal Mail
Jubilee Mail Ce...
First Class

SYDNEY

Sydney, Australia

I am writing to you from the Sanderson. Last night, as we
strolled home along the embankment we stopped for a
moment to watch a huge stingray silently drift beneath,
its' wings licking the stonework. I felt its presence.

My Love,
I am writing to you from
sunny & peaceful the
Tongariki. I am told
that these statues are
in fact coffins & tomb-
stones. Perhaps I am
being mislead, but I like
the idea. And hey, never
let facts get in the way of
a good story. ✗.

281216

Royal Mail
Jubilee Mail Centre
First Class

EASTER ISLAND

Easter Island

I am writing to you from sunny and peaceful Ahu Tongariki.
I am told that these statues are in fact coffins and tombstones.
Perhaps I am being misled, but I like the idea. And hey, never
let facts get in the way of a good story.

My Love,
I am writing to you from
the Parque Metropolitano
de Santiago. The boulevards
are wide, and the flowers,
bougainvillea, continue to
bloom. Every stray dog I
see I want to adopt.
I will see the year out
without you. I will
think of you as colours
fill the sky.   A

Royal Mail
Jubilee Mail Centre
First Class

CHILE

Santiago, Chile

I am writing to you from the Parque Metropolitano
de Santiago. The boulevards are wide, and the flowers,
bougainvillea, continue to bloom. Every stray dog I see
I want to adopt. I will see the year out without you.
I will think about you as colours fill the sky.

My Love,

I am in an un-pronounceable café near Skógar foss. These waterfalls, they're majestic. The nights are long, but I have not seen the northern lights. I am told that, rather unfortunately, I have come to see my friends during an unprecedented heat wave. It's 1°C.

200217   A.

Royal Mail
Jubilee Mail Centre
First Class

ICELAND

Iceland

I am in an un-pronounceable café near Skógafoss. These
waterfalls, they're majestic. The nights are long but I have
not seen northern lights. I am told that, rather unfortunately,
I have come to see my friends during an unprecedented heat
wave. It's 1 degree.

My Love,

I am writing to you from Café de la Paix. Everyone seems to be wearing white. I am wearing black, just less black than usual. I am confused as to why the Jardin de Tuileries isn't paved, and clouds of dust are allowed to rise as the wind blows. I am told the dust "adds character". Jury's out. A.

110617

Royal Mail
Jubilee Mail Cer :r.
First Class

PARIS

Paris, France

I'm writing to you from Café de la Paix. Everyone seems to be
wearing white. I am wearing black, just less black that usual.
I am confused as to why the Jardin de Tuileries isn't paved,
and clouds of dust are allowed to rise as the wind blows.
I am told the dust "adds character". Jury's out.

My Love,

I am writing to you from
the desert, my favourite
place on Earth. The
silence is consuming.
If I stand still I
can hear my heartbeat.
This is the origin of
my obscure sorrows.

170717   A.

Royal Mail
Jubilee Mail Centre
First Class

LAS VEGAS

Las Vegas, USA

I am writing to you from the desert, my favourite place on
Earth. The silence is consuming. If I stand still I can hear my
heartbeat. This is the origin of my obscure sorrows.

My Love,

Somewhere in Pasadena
a lock of my hair is in
an old flame's re-modelled
fireplace, in a fake brick.
He wrote me my first
love letter age 14. I
picked up his habit.

A.

230717

Royal Mail
Jubilee Mail Centre
First Class

LOS ANGELES

Los Angeles, July

Somewhere in Pasadena a lock of my hair is in an old flame's
re-modelled fireplace, in a fake brick. He wrote me my first
love letter age 14. I picked up his habit.

My Love,

On Wednesday you asked me why I liked you. I believe I can now answer that question in five words:
while others burn,
you shine.

That is all.   A.

100817

Royal Mail
Jubilee Mail C
First Class

IBIZA

Ibiza, Spain

On Wednesday you asked me why I liked you. I believe I can
now answer that question in five words: while others burn,
you shine. That is all.

My Love,

I am making a sit with my family at Florian's. Venice smells like seaweed, old socks & fresh coffee. The piazza is filled with music and merriment and I am quite content. I feel my hypothermia dissolving away. I am overcome with freedom & hope.

A.

041017

VENICE

Venice, Italy

I am making a sit with my family at Florian's. Venice smells
like seaweed, old books and fresh coffee. The piazza is filled
with music and merriment and I am quite content. I feel
my hypothermia dissolving away. I am overcome with
freedom and hope.

My Love,

I am having tea and torte at Café Central. I prefer the Imperial torte to the famed Sacher. It's the layers, it adds texture and amusement. I'm going to the Opera tonight. It's not a Wagner, but no matter. I'll still delight in the traditional powdered wigs and ornate set. A.

15 11 17
Royal Mail
Jubilee Mail Centre
First Class

VIENNA

Vienna, Austria

I am having tea and torte at Café Centraal. I prefer the
Imperial torte to the famed Sacher. It's the layers, it adds
texture and amusement. I'm going to the Opera tonight.
It's not a Wagner, but no matter. I'll still delight in the
traditional powdered wigs and ornate set.

My Love,

I am at the Yuen Po bird
market in Kowloon - it's
loud, but not unpleasant,
much like the rest of HK.
Hong Kong unfolds like
an accordion. These
aromatic delights have
blooming ends, enough
to have one's fill.

A.

14 12 17

Royal Mail
Jubilee Mail Centre
First Class

HONG KONG

Hong Kong, China

I am at the Yuen Po bird market in Kowloon – it's loud, but
not unpleasant, much like the rest of HK. Hong Kong unfolds
like an accordion. These aromatic delights have blooming
ends, enough to have one's fill.

My Love,

I'm at the Gunsite Café
by the Beaumont Tower.
Calling it a tower is
quite an embellishment.
But it's been standing
here, defending St.
Aubins since the 1780s,
so that's something.

A.

1 8 12 17
Royal Mail
Jubilee Mail Centre
First Class

JERSEY

Jersey, UK

I'm at the Gunsite Café by the Beaumont Tower. Calling it a
tower is quite an embellishment. But it's been standing here,
defending St Aubins since the 1780s, so that's something.

My Love,

I am writing to you from the Perez Museum of Art. It's raining but the pelicans are flying unfazed. I am eating a "deconstructed cheesecake". The rain won't last long. Neither will this cheesecake.

A.

29 12 17

Royal Mail
Jubilee Mail Centre
First Class

MIAMI

Miami, USA

I am writing to you from the Perez Museum of Art.
It's raining but the pelicans are flying unfazed. I am eating
a "deconstructed cheesecake". The rain won't last long.
Neither will this cheesecake.

My Love,

I am writing to you from my favourite place, where in January the sun is bright, the days are long and I get to watch the ocean waves break upon the serrated shoreline below. This would be better with you.

2 7 01 1 8   A.

Royal Mail
Jubilee Mail Centre
First Class

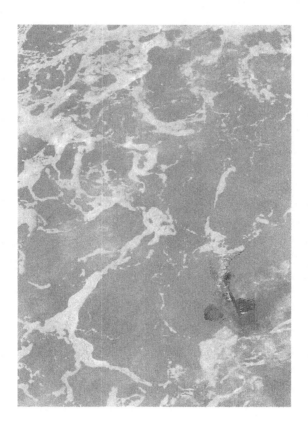

BERMUDA

Bermuda

I am writing to you from my favourite place, where in January
the sun is bright, the days are long and I get to watch the
ocean waves break upon the serrated shoreline below.
This would be better with you.

My Love,

You have gone to buy some
food, so I am quickly
writing this at the station.
Unfortunately, we are
at the wrong station,
and we have missed
our train to Venice.

But no matter, another
train departs in half an
hour. I also hope you
are buying me a snack,
for I am peckish.   A.

ROME

Rome, Italy

You have gone to buy some food so I am quickly writing this
at the station. Unfortunately, we are at the wrong station, and
we have missed our train to Venice. But no matter, another
train departs in half an hour. I also hope you are buying me
a snack, for I am peckish.

My Love,
The countryside is littered
with fatty geese. They are
just everywhere! The land
is flat as a pancake,
with little, peaceful ditches
dividing up the farmland.
Needless to say the fancy
birds can be spotted
easily, dressed in dazzling
white. I'm charmed.

A.

2 1 04 1 8
Royal Mail
Jubilee Mail Centr:
First Class

HOORN

Hoorn, Netherlands

In the town Square of Hoorn, I am having a coffee and am
slowly overdosing on stroopwaffles. It's cooler than expected
and my hands briefly lose feeling as I read those love letters
you gave me for my birthday. I hope you are well.

My Love,
The countryside is littered
with fatty geese. They are
just everywhere! The land
is flat as a pancake,
with little, peaceful ditches
dividing up the farmland.
Needless to say the fancy
birds can be spotted
easily, dressed in dazzling
white. I'm charmed.

A.

2 1 04 1 8
Royal Mail
Jubilee Mail Centr:
First Class

HOLLAND

Kinderdijk, Netherlands

The countryside is littered with fatty geese. They are just everywhere! The land is flat as a pancake with little, peaceful ditches dividing up farmland. Needless to say, the fancy birds can be spotted easily, dressed in dazzling white. I'm charmed.

My Love,

I'm eating waffles while digesting the view of The Cathedral of St. Michael and St. Gudula. I feel spring for the first time. It's especially evident given the surprisingly numerous green spaces in the city. The sky is cloudless and I feel rested.   A.   24 04 18

Royal Mail
Jubilee Mail Centre
First Class

BRUSSELS

Brussels, Belgium

I'm eating waffles while digesting the view of The Cathedral
of St. Michael and St. Gudula. I feel spring for the first time.
It's especially evident given the surprisingly numerous green
spaces in the city. The sky is cloudless and I feel rested.

My Love,
Spring has sprung in its
full beauty. I feel
embraced by the sun
once more, making me
feel eternal. And
Brugge is a wonderful
place to welcome it in.
Gentle echoes of hooves
on the cobbles, it's so
quiet here I could
hear a bee sneeze.
It's perfect.   A.

28 04 18
Royal Mail
Jubilee Mail Centre
First Class

BRUGGE

Brugge, Netherlands

Spring has sprung in its full beauty. I feel embraced by the
sun once more, making me feel eternal. And Brugge is a
wonderful place to welcome it in. Gentle echoes of hooves
on the cobbles, it's so quiet here I could hear a bee sneeze.
It's perfect.

My Love,
At the end of a last spring
day we watched the sun
set over Jerusalem. Gentle
shades of pink and peach
cascading into one
another with each passing
minute, turning lilac,
then violet. The call to
evening payer began and
echoed over the valley.
It was uplifting and
enchanting. A.

140518
Royal Mail
Jubilee Mail Cent
First Class

ISRAEL

Jerusalem, Israel

At the end of a hot spring day we watched the sun set over
Jerusalem, gentle shades of pink and peach cascading into one
another with each passing minute, tuning lilac, then violet.
The call to evening prayer began and echoed over the valley.
It was uplifting and enchanting.

My Love,
On the first floor of a
tea house, I am with
my mother, overlooking the
ancient columnar square.
As I looked out of the
window, I remarked
"it's raining". My mother
agreed. The following
silence was filled with the
delicate, muted splashes of
droplets on the stone slabs
outside. A.   26 05 18

Royal Mail
Jubilee Mail Centre
First Class

BATH

Bath, England

On the first floor of a tea house, I am with my mother,
overlooking the ancient columnar square. As I looked out
of the window I remarked "it's raining". My mother agreed.
The following silence was filled with the delicate, muted
splashes of droplets on the stone slabs outside.

My Love,
The air is fresh, yet warming.
Green and blue bunting,
stretched between lampposts
at the main harbour point,
is softly swaying in the
breeze. Shimmering
water laps the legion of
cosy, anchored boats.
Gentle hints of vinegar
linger in the air, promises
of fish and chips.

A.

FOWEY

Fowey, England

The air is fresh, yet warming. Green and blue bunting, stretched between lampposts at the main harbour point, is softly swaying in the breeze. Shimmering water laps the legion of cosy, anchored boats. Gentle hints of vinegar linger in the air, promises of fish and chips.

Made in the USA
Coppell, TX
26 October 2020

40291688R00072